Mail Carriers

Julie Murray

Abdo
MY COMMUNITY: JOBS
Kids

abdopublishing.com

Published by Abdo Kids, a division of ABDO, PO Box 398166, Minneapolis, Minnesota 55439.
Copyright © 2016 by Abdo Consulting Group, Inc. International copyrights reserved in all countries.
No part of this book may be reproduced in any form without written permission from the publisher.

Printed in the United States of America, North Mankato, Minnesota.

052015

092015

 THIS BOOK CONTAINS
RECYCLED MATERIALS

Photo Credits: AP Images, Canada Post, iStock, Landov Media, Shutterstock,
© LesPalenik p.22, Zvonimir Atletic p.22 / Shutterstock.com

Production Contributors: Teddy Borth, Jennie Forsberg, Grace Hansen

Design Contributors: Candice Keimig, Dorothy Toth

Library of Congress Control Number: 2014958406

Cataloging-in-Publication Data

Murray, Julie.
 Mail carriers / Julie Murray.
   p. cm. -- (My community: jobs)
ISBN 978-1-62970-915-4
Includes index.
1. Letter carriers--Juvenile literature.   I. Title.
383'.145--dc23
                    2014958406

Table of Contents

Mail Carriers

Mail carriers have a big job.

They deliver mail.

Jan gets a letter.

They pick up mail.

They take it to the post office.

They **sort** the mail.

They put mail in the truck.

And off they go!

Some mail carriers walk.

They use bags to carry the mail.

Carrying mail is hard.

It is heavy!

15

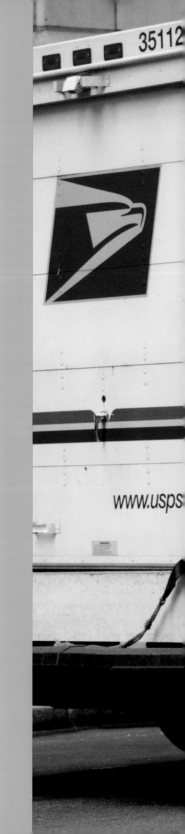

They wear **uniforms**.

They are blue and gray.

The mail comes six days a week. No mail on Sundays.

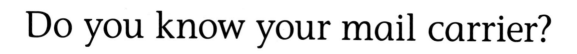
Do you know your mail carrier?

A Mail Carrier's Tools

mail bag

mailboxes

mail truck

stamps

Glossary

deliver

to take something to a person or place.

uniform

a type of clothing that is worn by all the members of a group or organization.

sort

the act of separating things and putting them in a particular order.

Index

abdokids.com

Use this code to log on to abdokids.com and access crafts, games, videos, and more!

Abdo Kids Code:
MMK9154

24